Some Things Gentle
Some Things Kind

the poetry of
CRAIG WILLIAM ANDREWS

Some Things Gentle
Some Things Kind

An effulgent publication of
AUTUMN SUN PUBLISHING
Sequim, Washington

Some Things Gentle
Some Things Kind
by Craig William Andrews

Copyright © 2014 by Craig William Andrews
All rights reserved.
Printed in the United States of America

Published by
Craig Andrews / Autumn Sun Publishing
tarasparkman@yahoo.com

Typestyle: Sabon
Book Design by Ruth Marcus, Rmarcus@olypen.com
Illustration on Half Title Page by Craig William Andrews

No part of this book may be used or reproduced in any manner whatsoever without the written permission of the author.

ISBN 978-0692263-66-2

Dedication

For Tara.
My fierce editor,
and Song of My Heart.
After 23 years,
our marriage is always,
"just begun."

Table of Contents

xi	PREFACE
xv	THEME
1	THE WALK
3	INDRAS NET
4	I DREAM
5	DRAGONS IN MIST AND FOAM
6	SEARCHLIGHT
8	THE NATURE OF THE MYSTERY
11	CALIOPE
14	SILHOUETTE IN DAWN
15	COMING HOME
16	THE BECKENING
17	REDEMPTION OF A POET
20	MATILIJA THE MOTHER SHIP
22	IN DAWNING SUMMERS FLIGHT
24	COMMUNITY
26	THE MYSTERY OF MYSELF
28	THE LONG ABIDING SELF
30	I AND I
31	THIS TREE OF LIFE
34	WE ARE

40	RIDING MY WIND
41	VALENTINES DAY
42	A SONG IN BAMBOO
43	IN THE LIGHT OF YOGA
45	IN MEMORIAL: THE PEOPLE'S PARK
47	TWO OF A KIND
48	BIRTH OF A DRAGON
49	HOMAGE
50	ARIA
52	ABORUS
53	IN PLIGHTING MINE TROTH TO THEE
54	GERMANE
55	I WISH TO EMPTY THE COFFERS OF MY IGNORANCE
56	THE TRANSCENDENTALIST
57	HOLOGRAM

Preface

Allow me to enthuse upon you; That I love being a Poet. I love weaving thoughts and feelings, patterns and rhythms, like the warp and weft of a carpet. And the Field, like music, perhaps like carpets, is very large.

There is a "Free Form" which runs loose in this Field. A Free Form of Poetry. There is also a Free Form in Music, and though I doubt, there is possibly a Free Form in Rugs? I do not know, but it is here that I love to fly.

I envision my Muse as running through my Creative Fields; laughing, playing, Being in Love. She is essentially free, comes to me in my easy chair and whispers in my ear, "You need to paint the house."

"I have never painted a house," I reply.

"That's okay, I'll help you."

"Ok, if that's what you want."

And then I paint the house in four colors, and it is beautiful.

My Muse can come as anything, but mostly, these days, she comes as poems. Sometimes she will lay a poem out before me so that all I need to do is

transcribe and lace on my "own" finishing touches. I do not feel like I am cheating while other poets sit for hours with a vacant mind. If my mind is vacant it is because she is off exploring other parts of my psyche and I need to wait until she returns. Patience is my staff.
If I use it to smite the ground, water will appear.

Theme

In the Beginning:
The Daughters of the Silver Light
Gathered Moonstones from the pebbles which lay
    by the sea,
And the Brothers of the Golden Orb
Took the Crystals from the Mountains,
It is the Janus face of who we are;
One body looking in two directions,
One Heart with two minds,
It is who we are.

The Walk

This morning
Like all mornings,
Shall begin with "The Walk"
The wife, my self, the dogs
Heading out along the path of our constitutional
The same path that we have walked three-hundred
    and sixty-five days of this year
In Spring and Summer, Winter and Fall,
Icy or hot,
Through wind and snow or pelting rain,
Sometimes fast and sometimes slow,
Sometimes before the rising of the day,
Happy or sad,
Walking through joy, or anger, or grief,
With injuries, or feeling sick, or having a spat
    with each other,
And there are deer, or coyotes, racoons, puma, eagle,
    or bear, ravens and all other birds galore,
Or there is our cat Farley, who would like to come but
    can't because sometimes there are crazy drivers
And somebody will need to carry him home,
There are plants which grow green and flower
And then they die,

And there are wild flowers of all kinds
And great big trees which sometimes drop limbs
    in storms
And all the sounds and smells are never the same,
As if we are always coming to a different place,
And so the things we find along the road or the path,
Sometimes we need to "scoop the poop" from an
    inappropriate place,
Sometimes we need to scoop the beer cans from last
    nights yahoo drivers,
There is talk and new ideas and yelling at the dogs
    "Come Here!"
And I have come to think, that this Walk,
Like every day of my life,
Will never, ever, be the same,
For even as the sands of one moment fall into the glass
    of another
Nature does not know how to be the same,
That this Walk could lead us anywhere,
This walk could lead us to the Moon.

Indra's Net

This morning I stepped into Fall's Dewish Sunrise
And beheld Indra's Net
Glistening on every plant of purple sage and
    yellow lupine
The sun casting rainbows and bluewhite stars
Through every jeweled juncture of Time and Space,
The immensity of the Beauty and Perfection
Captured in that one eternal kiss of Now
Struck me with such force as to take my breath
And leave me helpless in this miracle
                            This wonder
Which for the Grace of God
Need not be at all,
And I swear unto all which is Divine
That I will never
Ever
See my Earth
My life,
In the same way again.

I Dream

I Dream,
On a warm afternoon,
Or cozy before a winter's fire
I settle into my chair
And I walk into other worlds,
Worlds which are marked by my name alone
Although it is perhaps, not the same name,
And I watch myself
Though I do not, perhaps, wear this same Earth suit,
But I perform deeds there,
And when I return to my chair
I am confused,
Which one of me
I wonder,
Was it that had this dream.

Dragons of Mist and Foam

Sunlight through rain
Like fire in water
A curtain of falling radiance,
And it is in this coupling
This coming to mix and meet
Like diamonds which dance upon the sea
That Dragons are born,
The Yang birthed in Yin
Fire in Water
To travel as a brilliance through the veins of my people
And illuminate the world
With the power to freely vision
Upon the shards of scientific thought.

Searchlight

Could it be that Light was once a wandering Spirit?
Was once in search of its own identity
That it traveled from Darkness to Darkness
And from Void to Void,
And that it would find a place to sojourn from its
    quest But the
Darkness always drew away from it
And would not allow it in,
That it would curl-up in the bottom of the Void and
    find its rest
But the Void was without a bottom
And it had no walls,
So The Light would find itself outside when it thought
    itself in,
And would not know how that came to be,
But it also did not know that every Darkness
    was the same Darkness,
And that every Void was the same Void
And that as the Darkness fled from it
A Dawn began to unfold, (Did I just do That?)
Or that the Void, Being Void,

Was what allowed The Light "To Be,"
For The Light was Pure Intelligence,
It had no words, and it had no life
It could be anything at all

But it had to wait to be noticed,
It had to wait for Me to evolve.

The Nature of the Mystery

It is Life which is the Gateway to the Mystery...
The Big Momma/Poppa Mystery
The Prime Mystery
Which comes through when Life looks into Its Self
And sees its Self smiling back in the Bliss of Its
    own Ineffability,
Smiling from the place of Its own Impossibility
Because Life is Impossible,
Why is there anything at all?
How can Worlds come from Nothing?
This is an Absurdity which drives me to write this poem
And it is in traveling through the landscape of this poem
That it occurs to me
That it is really nothing less than Divine Being
Which is birthed through this Basic Absurdity that we
    call Life
Because The Mystery, The Really Big Mystery
Cannot exist until some consciousness,
Somewhere,
Takes note of its existence,
Quantum Mechanics then defines the first rule for
    meeting God,

You need to notice Him-Her-It,
And Life itself actually has no basis for existence,
Being that you cannot step aside from your life to
    see your life
Life has no backdrop to show itself off,
No support
No ground or foundation in any direction,
It has no reason and no possibility of Being at all!

This can only leave us with some kind of omnipresence,
Of which "God" is the accepted generic term,
And this is important,
Because there is no other word which could lay down
    in comfort
Hands behind Its head
Within this impossibility!
And because of the generic quality of this word,
God can be anything,
Anywhere,
Anytime,
And do so with a Power and a Poise which
    boggles our ability to ken

And all of this with no effort at all!
And this then IS The Mystery,
Which begets The Mysteries
Because,
And this is also important,
If God is The Mystery
And God, by generic definition, is everything,
Then everything is a Mystery
And if everything is a Mystery
Then we can understand how something works
And we can give it a name
But we can never understand what it is
And this does seem to be the case,
Why then, I wonder,
Am I so involved in asking these questions?

Caliope

Where are we going?
Singing, laughing, shoving, loving,
Careening down the corridors of Time
Clearly out of control
Fighting, biting, discovering, birthing,
We need to know,
We demand to understand,
We tear it apart!
Savage it to see how it works,
But then we can't put it back together again
And cry and want it whole and new, and untrammeled
And poison ourselves for comfort
Or writhe in ecstasy delivered by our mind
Drop by drop
To open our perception to vistas of Eternity
And our Heart to Peace,
Yet still we may ask,
Why are we doing this at all?
To prove what?
To get where?
To dance on the hot coals of some Demi-God?
For what reason?

Why do we need to know?
Do we need to know?
What would become of us if we did not ask these
    questions?
What if nothing became of us?
Nothing at all,
If we lived stupid to the questions,

If we did not need pride?
If we were not fearful for our comfort?
If we did not covet what another had found
Be it love, or health, or gold?

It has been said, "Those who seek will find."
And "Finding" will find that nothing has been found
For it is not as if pieces of our psyche lay scattered
    about the Fields of Life
A treasure hunt for Wholeness
Like finding Easter Eggs under leaves
And eating them suddenly become Whole –
    Enlightened?
And then what do we do?

What if "Finding" we find the game is over?
The game over and now there is truly no place to go
And nothing to do?
The Zen Master chops wood, carries water, and throws
   a tennis ball for his Labrador.

Silhouette in Dawn

There are times when I feel no anger,
When all my Past seems only a road that I have
    traveled on
Sometimes through the darkest and the scariest
    places wherein my mind could dwell,
Other times, traveled to our trysting place
Where Life is Joy in Being Life
Filled with airy places
The lightness of Light
The weaving of Songs
So that Kali's Skulls
Shake like maracas
And Her bare feet beat in time with the tabla
And Her hands clap the becoming of worlds
Infinity dances within Her smile
And "Now" is the only word we intone
In all of our poems.

Coming Home

Q. Did they ship the body home?
A. The body was an Earthling,
   He was already home,
Q. But surely the deceased must have come from
   Someplace else?
   He was not one of us,
A. The deceased, born of this world, was surely one of us,
   Delivered into our care,
   He did not live beyond the Vale,
Q. But surely there are those who will miss him?
   Friends and family who will want him back?
A. We will send the body to where they wait,
   They will dress him and fondle him,
   Weep and suffer their loss,
   And a small girl will find a little dead bird in the
   driveway of the funeral home,
   And without thought,
   In a basic sense of what is true to life,
   She will carefully place it beneath a tree,
   And the tree will welcome it Home.

The Beckoning

I Am a Swan,
My arms are wings
My neck is long,
I Am powerful
Free,

Somewhere far below is the steady beat of the
    Drum
But I Am not that person,
My skin has cracked and fallen away
And I have flown into the Faerie skys of Eld,
Have you seen me?
Perhaps in that space between sleep and waking
    dream?

I Am your promise
But I Am also my truth.

Redemption of a Poet

Canto I

No!
I can not do this!
I cannot sit at my desk in orderly time
Nor in orderly fashion!
This is not writing a poem
This is composing a poem,
A letter, an essay, or a story,
This is like building a poem from Lincoln Logs,
Constructing Beauty,
It can be done, but I will not do it,
I will ever be free,
My poetry must always burst out from my Heart,
Rip open my chest and open my eyes,
The feel of the pen in my fingers
Like holding on to the tail feathers of a Dragon
My poem shall soar through the skys of
    unreasonable hope
Flaunting a naked majesty
And unblushingly wander in the Mythological
    byways of childlike wonder

For I am caught in the transcendental joy of my
    Natural life
My Muse singing to me out of worlds beyond
    redemption
I Am a Poet!
I Am not a composer of words!

Canto II

The language is always a poor cousin to the pen
The pen is always searching for the word,
Crossing-out,
Doodling in the margins,
Reaching for the word which will never be found in
    the spell-check of any computer,
Birthing a word through the loins of my fervor,
Confabulating with beings of Light and beings of
    Shadow
Who inhabit the woodsy areas of my mind
Tempting me to expose myself in Public places,
Back rooms which are pirate dens of Poets
Who would take those who compose,
Strip them bare and force them with the pointed end
    of an implement of cursive expression

To walk the plank of their own trepidation
And fall into the wild places of their Heart.

Canto III

To place the poetry of another as unbeautiful,
    unlovely, or dismeaningful,
Would be to place my own creative art in jeopardy,
I cannot be the Judge and Jury of Creation
I Am too close to it all
Too intertwined into the Bacchanal of Earthly Existence:

To objectify the passion of another person
Would be to tear the flesh from my own art
And leave me bleeding in contempt of my own lineage
For there is room for us all,
I shall write,
Others shall compose.

Matiltija the Mother Ship

It's the Light!
Like a small sun,
But no yellow
No white or orange or blue,
Just an absolutely pure clear light
So brilliant that it hurts your eyes to gaze into it for
    more than a moment or two,
And you can vaguely make out the shape of it through
    the intensity of its radiation,
It has six wings that may be crystal
And a body of gold
Shined and buffed and true to color almost to the
    highlights of white
Incorruptible
Your breath is taken away by the intensity of it all,
Gold tendrils extend from the golden body to the lights
And there is a flood light on the bottom of its
    central cylinder,
A landing light,
It hovers above the table in the living room
And may be an Alien Mother ship artfully disguised
    as a chandelier

Which stealthily placed itself within the confines of the
    "Waste-Not-Want-Not" store
And advertised itself for only ten dollars so that we
    would take it home

It is a Swan in its Beauty!
Too Perfect,
Too luminous to be what it says it is,
I am waiting for it to communicate,
Perhaps on some dark and stormy Winter's night,
And in the morning people will come to find the house
    empty
And the chandelier gone.

In Dawning Summers Flight

It is love which has given these wings to me,
That this world, to my Soul, is sprightly brought
And comely to my sight,
And that my heart could not contrive
To show more Beauty when I rise
Than the loveliness of your smile
Nor the sparkling of the light
That captures my breath
In the opening of your Irish eyes,
And in the songs of the greening leaves
And the silences of the snows
Through the aging of our life
The Enchantment fairly grows,
Ah! My girl
My likely lass,
Let's not leave this Sacred world
When Heaven calls at last,
Not repair to Elysium Fields where trouble
    never lies
But place our wraith into the Earth
The fields, the streams, and skies,
And the power which bades the stars to move

To pace the Hall of Time
Through the Oaken Door
Shall shod anew
Our bodies young and fine.

Community

Today I have driven me to that large open space also
 known as our Wal+Mart parking lot,
I have parked on the far edge where the RV's spread
 their tires for the night,
There, I removed my person from the cab of my pick-
 up truck
Sat my mug of coffee upon the hood
And for a goodly amount of time
Gazed at a parade of spring clouds
Chasing each other across a vastness of blue
Accented by the blackness of asphalt and the colors
 of cars,
And from where I stand I listen as the wind sings a
 powerfully beautiful song through the pines which
 form the forest that runs between the parking lot
 and the golf course which, in itself, forms another
 kind of vastness
A vastness of manicured green,
And the dogs pee and poop and chase mice in the wild
 grass which grows between the curb of the parking
 lot and a line of yellow lupine

Lupine that has grown ornamental in its tantric dance
    with time, concrete, and aluminum cans
While high above
An Eagle traces a lazy circle in the April sky.

The Mustering of Myself

Who, I sometimes wonder, do I write these poems for?
For "you" who I do not know?
For my wife? Yes, sometimes,
For my self so that I may read the intricate loveliness
    of my own words?
I Am, after all, my own third party,
I marvel at the ingenuity, the insight,
The deeply layered meanings of my own lyrics
As if I am reading a poet who I have just now
    discovered,
Somebody who I have yet to know
And perhaps there is some truth in this?
But truly, I write these poems to open doors
And they are open to everybody
To everything
To walk through,
For they simply open doorways scattered across the
    fields of the Mind
And they are only there to lead to questions
The same questions that other writers have asked,
Forever,
Since the beginning of Time,

And these doors do not lead to answers
Because there are no answers to these questions,
They, like us, are simply endlessly alive,
To answer them would be to kill them
And then the whole Universe would have to die,
It would have to die because God is a Poet
And only lives in The Questions
And yes, of course, in the Beauty which fills my eyes.

The Long Abiding Self

The Buddha said that there is no Self,
No individual and long abiding Soul,
No Self to be a part of this Mother World,
And so who was it, I wonder?
Who stood before the village door
Empty bowl in hand,
And who was it then that filled that bowl with rice
Asked for a blessing upon her home
And laughed in the joy of seeing her child take its first
    uncertain steps into this magical world,
And where is the Spring of this loveliness The headwaters
    of this river which flows through the human heart
To flood our worldly Nature
Our greater Self
Expressed as all things green, or feathered,
Or covered with fur,
And reflected back to me in the soft eyes of my beloved
As we cozy together before a winter's fire
And read the words of other gifted Souls
For I am certain that the Buddha knew,
Must have known
That there is one Soul
Artfully disguised as a burgeoning bubbling

Long abiding Self
Rising to the surface of its own Infinite Freedom
The Great Kindness of its own Spirit
To be able to stumble and fall and feel the pain
Of forever becoming one individualized flower
In the bouquet of Life

Fed and nourished by the myriad composted bodies
    of non-abiding Selves
Which fall like rain
Onto the ground of Being
As lives shed lives to live the One Life
My own True Self
Gifted as Light from the loins of Shiva
Into the womb of Maya
To birth this World made only for the sensual feast
To Dance the Dance
And Sing the Song
I Am That I Am Me.

I and I

I Am posing as an Enlightened Soul,
For if I play my part well
And believe in the part that I Am playing
I will no longer need to be
An Enlightened Soul.

This Tree of Life

Eternity, by definition, has no beginning and no End,
It has only Centers,
For any point in Eternity is surrounded by Eternity,
It has no place to go
No place to travel to
So each and every thing which resides in Eternity
Is the Center of its own Universe,
And although Eternity can only be a Center
With no up, and no down,
No sides or corners or edges,
This Center, which is Me, is HUGE
And as I explore Me I find other Centers living Here
They are all contained in Me and they are all doorways
    into their own HUGE Self which contains Me,
And so there is no possibility that I will ever reach
  the end of my Self
And yet I Am only a leaf
I Am one leaf
I Am one leaf on one small branch which has leaves all
    the way to my horizon
And each leaf on this small branch is a human being
Or the idea of a human being
And there is a branch for every different thing

Which is the Center of its own Universe but only one leaf
 upon its own branch
And all of these branches join to a limb
And there are limbs beyond my count which join to the
 trunk of this tree
Limbs which reach into the Crown beyond all of my
 ability to imagine,

And the trunk travels down through whole Universes and
 into its roots
Which curl about the bottom of its own Center
Where they drink from the Spring of Life
Which in true artesian fashion
Gushes forth from Eternity,
For if Eternity has a Name
Then Eternity has a presence,
And if Eternity has a presence
Then Eternity has a personality,
And if Eternity has a personality
Then Eternity drinks from a Soul,
So the Tree of Life is gifted from Eternity
An act of Love which grows into worlds and Universes
 of worlds,

Life flowing up the trunk and into the limbs
Out to the branches and into my Center
Which is the leaf of Me
That comes as a Rose
And the dew on my petals
Are the tears of my joy,
For I will never reach the end of my Beauty
On this tree whose leaves have just begun.

We Are

We Are ground
The Earth reflects in our eyes
There is a Greenness to our thoughts
Nurtured in a Loving Kindness
Which is our Covenant to All,
We Are the sound of Laughter
The Flight of Birds
A creative Beauty
From the Eternal Spring of our Life
Through our Heart Into our World,
Musing, A-Musing,
Playing in the Elysium Fields of our joy
Bringing Wonder into the lives that we touch
We Are Blessed with an abundance of all good things
Wrapping our self about the Pole of our togetherness
We Are Ananda
We throw open the Gate to "Yes!"

The Mayan Calendar

There is a wind which is blowing across the Fields

There are winds which cross the surface of our world
Some of these are famous winds
Winds with names like
Sirocco, Santa Ana, or Mistral,
Dangerous, angry winds like, Tornadoes, Gales, and hurricanes,
Winds which carry devils to taunt our fortitude
And winds which dance and play
Soothe and refresh,
The Zephyr which shyly teases our senses,
Soft Summer Breezes which tickle our fancy carrying the sweet scent of flower blossoms
And tumble us into love,

Aeolus, you see, is a fickle God
Unpredictable, enigmatic,
And all of the winds are Spirits of his moods,
And what are we?
To be kissed, caressed, or torn into pieces of flying debris?

For all winds, any wind, is a Spirit beyond our ken,
They sport in this Maya
In which we so seriously seek to make our gain.

Ah, But this wind which is moving through us now
Is not a wind of that kind
Not that ilk or humor,
It is a wind particular to the inner life of the Soul
For the Soul is not not a fixed point in the flow of
 Eternity
But an ever expanding, ever enriching "I"
Which seeks to include all of existence into its Being
And this wind blows through all of the Souls
And turns them in a new direction,
Reshapes their desires and their dreams
And brings them into Day 1, Reed 1
In this new cycle of the Earth.

Solstice

I have blessed this poem with Eagle Feather
With the smoke of Sage
Because it is a Medicine Poem
A Message Poem
That it may have Wings
To fly the shape of my Heart
The content of my Words
My language Song
To the lodge of my Father
And knock on the Door
Whos' Soul made Me
That He will fly down on Eagle Wings
And fill all the dark places of my Mind
With the light of my own returning Sun
My Solstice of Healing
Through Love
Just Come.

Solstice II

The warmth has gone from my world,
It happens every year
It has left me to travel in far flung lands
Where the Sun still rides high,
A golden horse with wild eyes
And hoofs which strike sparks
That rain down into the open arms of greening life
Whist I curl-up
Closed-off and alone
Dreaming of the smells of hot fir and pine
Grieving this season of loss
Keening through the darkness of my thoughts
Straining to hear the light steps of Solstice
My Lady of Returning Light,
Yea, that my heart may bud
And Reach into new life
Once again.

Solstice III

Rocks so cold
That if you brushed against them
They would open the flesh in gaping wound
Which would not heal
Until the lizards released from Saurian Dreams
Become targets once again
For speeding vehicles
On a Summer's Solstice Night.

Riding In My Wind

My mind is a wind
Which blows unseen through worlds,
I Am a Swan
Riding in my wind
Searching for the world I left behind,
But I Am a Dragon
Born of Air and Sea
Into this world of teaming life
Clutching to me
Hungry for comfort,
Hungry for love,
I gather it in,
In the Name of Compassion
In the Power of the Word,
But when I fly,
When I Am a Swan in the wind,
I must open my arms
And allow them to be wings
Once again,
And what I have held
I must allow to gently drop.

Valentine's Day

I know that this Universe is here by Intelligent Design
Because no random sampling of apples
Could ever have evolved a National Holiday
Celebrating the beauty of Love and Friendship
Just so,
Only so,
I could give a chocolate kiss
To you, my Lass
And hold you in my arms
And realize that our journey into Forever
Is always "just begun."

A Song in Bamboo

There is a flute resting on my lips
And the pure, sweet tones which it plays
Journey through my breath from the gracious Heart
    of this Earth
A Faerie song sung through the Soul of grass,
And it is this Soul of grass which whispers to the wind
The hauntingly beautiful refrains,
Brahmin's gift
To the first Dawn of Time
His Song sung for His love of Her
Which birthed worlds through Her loins
Flowers of Life,
Captured within the Enchantment of Her
This spell of the Poem Primordial
The purity of a green and vibrant song
Born naked of our words
Which divide us and hold us apart,
The Magic and Miracle of my fingers
Which dance upon the holes
Burned into this gift of grass
To play a tune of rocks and trees
And Beauty's kiss of Eternity.

In The Light of Yoga

I Am standing in the center of my self
Balanced
My bare feet snug into the nap of a Chinese carpet,
My spine is straight
Extended,
My chin is tucked
I Am a study in silence
I Am waiting to move,
I Am standing in a tradition which reaches back
    before recorded time,
Behind me there flows a river of Being
Yogis and yoginis poised to move from a still center
    into the focused position of asana
A physical joining to the sanctity of Life
Which has bequeathed to me the lineage of my Path;
Before me there extends Souls into infinity
Each poised,
Waiting to enter into the practice of sensual
    moving joy;
I Am the center of this focus,
All radiates out from me,
Like spokes from the hub of a wheel
I Am still while the Universe turns

Shiva dancing in the Heart of the World to the beat
    of the tabla,
I raise my arms
Feeling every hair alive in their passage through air
Bringing the palms of my hands together high above
    my head
I drift down into namaste,

I Am proud and humble
Gifted and Blessed to have this Practice,
Breathing into my movement
I Am a Sacred Chalice of inspiration,
I stretch into position and hold posture,
Sometimes it seems as if the Earth were the yogin
    and I was the asana,
And this yoga, my moving Path,
Is the becoming of our Truth
The Earth and I,
And as I strengthen both my mind and my body
My song and my beauty
I Am reminded of the promise given so long ago,
That one day Human-Beings shall radiate Light
Like unto Heaven
Which shall fall as kindness into the roots of the Earth
And Her own yoga shall shine as a Star.

In Memorial: The People's Park

I was there
When 70 thousand of us
Marched down Telegraph Avenue
In Berkeley, California
And the local radio station
Played "The Dawning of the Age of Aquarius"
Over and over and over again
And the people placed their radios
On The window ledges above the street
While young girls danced down the asphalt
Placing daisy's into the muzzels of guns
Held at ready by National Guardsmen
Who were only boys themselves
Wide eyed and trembling
In front of concertina wire
And mothers and fathers
Walked with children on their shoulders
While their dogs played about their feet
And the Power of the people
Was felt into the Halls of the Mighty
Who could only watch
And wait
And in the end would have their way

But could not know
And could not feel
That the Earth had spoken that day

That it was not victory which mattered
But the voice of Infinite Sentient Beings
The "Meek," which was Foretold
And rolled down our cheeks
As tears
Washing away
Washing away
The thousands of years of fear
That it takes to become Human.

Two of a Kind

It is my ability to feel with you,
My sympathy for your pain,
How I hurt when you hurt
That allows you to have a friend,
And the joy I feel in your joy
And our laughter together
Which transcends all dullness of Heart,
For it is in feeling together that we know our kind,
Know what it is to be Human,
Walking that razors edge
Which leads us from now
Through the Gateway of the Moon.

Birth of a Dragon

There is no Magic in a world
Where the Heart does not believe
And this is perhaps our greatest sorrow
For it is only through Magic that joy sojourns,
Maya
The Breath of God
Which brings Life into the merely living
And color into gray,
Luminescence – Opalescence,
The fall of a leaf
And the destiny of a new love
By Magic are born,
Lila dancing on the head of a pin,
Look closely and the pin becomes a World,
For verily our life is a wish fulfilling gem,
Our desires birth things,
Our wishes birth life-times,
Our thoughts are wings,
And our ears become an ocean,
Cradled in Beauty
Lifted in Kindness
Through the Nature of our Truth,
Apprentice Dragons,
We have just begun

Homage

"I have come to bring you back with me
Back into the center of your practice,"
If I could do this much
If I could reconnect lost
Souls to their Practice
To their yoga which they have forgotten
Or left behind,
If I could place them into that Pure Land of thought/feeling
Where Heart and Mind are both partners in one reality
Then I would feel very good indeed!
I would be a Spiritual "Catcher in the Rye,"
And my time in this world wouldn't be for naught,
And the people would relax and sigh
And they would say,
"Thank you, Thank you. Why did I ever leave?"
If I could do those things,
And I would be a great winged bird
A crane graceful and free
Who flys through worlds
And alights in the ancient temple of my birth
And my ageless teacher would smile to see me arrive,
    Holding me abreast
And looking me in the eyes
He would say,
"Ah, you have done well indeed."

Aria

On this cold Winter's night
It is time to gather-in more wood for a warm
    and hungry fire,
I wrap myself into my coat
Flip on the light above the deck
And sliding open the glass door
Slip into the Elemental,
It has begun to snow
I Am walking into an Enchanted Ream,
Carefully I descend the steps from the deck to the earth
The light faintly luminous into the deepening silent black
Turn my head upward and the snow is born there
Only feet above my eyes
Coming from blackness into light
Floating down as individual crystalline flakes
To softly land upon my face
A swiftly melting kiss of winter's delight,
And then, responding to a call for comfort that I failed
    to heed before I left the house
I opened the door to my personal anatomy
To the Nature from whence it was born
And stood there
A magnificent Human Being,

Face to Heaven
Arms open wide in supplication
The warm fluids of my life
Striking the frozen ground beneath my feet
With steam rising back into the Celestial Realms
And I say to the Spirit who brought me to this home
Ah! Life is good!

Aborus

It is on nights like this that they come fully alive,
A sophistic phrase
As if thy were otherwise dank of mind,
But on these nights you can feel them,
The air cool and damp from rain,
Bright moon and promenading clouds;

For more than a hundred years they have been watching
    over this house and this vale in which we live,
More than a hundred years of whispering through these
    nights of power,
Knowing the fate of their brothers
Feeling their vibrations which travel through the earth,
Knowing the capricious knot in Human thinking,
But just as they were here together with those who
    have gone before
(The previous owner lived to be 105 in this very house.)
So we are together now in this new dance
This Magic Summoning of dark, and Air, and Moon;

How long do I have
I wonder,
To learn to speak in tree,
In the dialects of Fir and Spruce, and Pine.

In Plighting Mine Troth to Thee

I came into this world a trickle,
A remembrance dribbling down from
Some lofty height –
Unimaginable,
To become a laughing rill
Leaping from stone to stone
Gathering speed
Deepening in experience,
And became a stream,
Weighted now by what came to live in me,
Slowed by the responsibility of my forest,
Until in meeting you we became our river
Of great strength/flowing in our truth
Through lands of sudden immensity
Into a sea/dancing in the sparkling diamond light
Of our Dreams;

Ah, Lassie,
This poem for my promise,
For I Am mixed in you.

Germane

I Am here once again
Dumb founded
Watching this poem birth through my mind
Like watching words pass through a veil
Which separates a darkness from the Light of Me
Maya,
A seeming which only has substance within my sight,
For I do not know what I Am Not,
And I am not sure that I would exist at all if I did not
    have the words to describe myself to me,
And so it must be
That the teachers of the Dumb
Are Shining Beings,
Bestowers of life! – Gardeners of Souls,
Growing Souls from Darkness
So that some Great and most basic Thing
Could travel the deep and inexplicable Halls
To part the Veil
In this most grand seance that we call Earth
And dance into the Light
As a poem
Birthing me into the Brilliance of you.

I Wish to Empty the Coffers of My Ignorance

I wish to empty the coffers of my ignorance,
For there is a Beauty,
A wisdom,
Which I can no longer ignore,
I await the blossoming of my Truth,
I long to turn this long quandarous day of my life
Into the shortest day in this year of my Being,
Place it behind me
And turn to embrace this one Enchanted Moment
Of who I Truly Am,
The Magic of my Flower
A bloom too vast for my Earthly eyes to see
I must feel into its immensity
Into the Breath of Me
Your Breath Sweet Brahma Lord;

One exhale into Forever,
One inhale back into Eternity.

The Transcendentalist

When one, as a diversity of One,
A wave upon the Ocean of Life
Keenly aware of what it is not
In a Me-ness infinitely large,
Ever expanding,
Being the new foundation of its' own Sacred Being,
Finds its' Self
Moving away from the intensity of its own small theater
Its mini-act of the Soul
Which struts and suffers upon the stage of its own
    Mythological World
Playing all of the parts in the complexity of its own story
Encompassing life-times beyond count,
Arrives at one first small step
Which faces away from the ecstasy and the pain
And leaps into the air as a great winged bird
Wings pushing upon the buoyancy of space
Rising as a comet returning Home
Watching the quickly receding stew of Earthly passions
Fade away into the light of a New Day,
A Phoenix Dawn rising from out of its own ashes
To enfold all of Pasts' meannesses
Into a rectification of Naught
Having never been
For it was always just a story
Except for the bird Freely Flying
Twix that world and this.

Hologram

We are sleeping Dragons
Dreaming of Mornings' Flight,
Dozing before Times' Fire
Which burns in the Great Hall of Eternity
Forever consuming the Present
The Enchantment of Now
A flower of infinite petals
Stretching away forever like Indra's Net
Each petal the One True Center
The Holistic Dot which contains everything
Sees everything
Knows everything as Me.

OTHER BOOKS
BY
CRAIG WILLIAM ANDREWS

A Song In Amber

Acts of Creation

www.ingramcontent.com/pod-product-compliance
Lightning Source LLC
Chambersburg PA
CBHW022124040426
42450CB00006B/837